GW00535791

War-torn
Portsmouth
— THEN, AFTER AND NOW —

War-torn Portsmouth

— THEN, AFTER AND NOW —

ROBERT HIND

HALSGROVE

First published in Great Britain in 2016

Copyright © Robert Hind 2016

All rights reserved. No part of this publication may be reproduced,
stored in a retrieval system, or transmitted in any form or by any
means without the prior permission of the copyright holder.

British Library Cataloguing-in-Publication Data
A CIP record for this title is available from the British Library

ISBN 978 0 85704 288 0

HALSGROVE
Halsgrove House,
Ryelands Industrial Estate,
Bagley Road, Wellington, Somerset TA21 9PZ
Tel: 01823 653777   Fax: 01823 216796
email: sales@halsgrove.com

Part of the Halsgrove group of companies
Information on all Halsgrove titles is available at: www.halsgrove.com

Printed and bound in China by Everbest Printing Investment Ltd

Introduction and Foreword

At the end of the Second World War, the *Portsmouth Evening* News published a booklet titled *Smitten City*. Inside were some 120 photographs of the city of Portsmouth taken during and after the blitz.

Most of what happened in Portsmouth was never known during the war as it was the home to the largest naval dockyard in the world and, of course, the home of the Royal Navy, so the news was heavily censored.

Any documentaries showing archive footage and history programmes on the television mention London, Coventry, Southampton and Birmingham but never Portsmouth.

I know my mother who was bombed out from Diamond Street, Southsea as a girl aged twelve used to get so upset when watching these programmes and Portsmouth was never mentioned. 'Well, what about Portsmouth then!' she used to shout at the television almost in tears remembering the devastating times she lived through.

Although the city was not devastated as much as others, on the night of 10/11 January, 1941 the Luftwaffe did its worst. Principal shopping centres were obliterated,

several wonderful churches burnt to the ground and the beautiful Guildhall gutted. It took until 1959 for it to be back in use, opened by the Queen.

The fire raid of that January night caused 28 major fires with 2214 others raging, mostly unchecked because of broken water mains. 3000 people were made homeless and 171 killed. Of the 70,000 properties Portsmouth had in 1939, raid damage was recorded on over 80,000 properties as some were damaged two or three times.

When one considers the loss of life in such places as Tokyo, 100,000 in a single night, 9/10 March, 1945 and Dresden 35,000 recognisable corpses and an estimate of 350,000 in all on the night of 13/14 February, 1945. Portsmouth escaped, if that is the word, lightly with fewer than 1000 dead over the five years of war.

It is easy to say 'They started it, we'll finish it' and let them reap the whirlwind. Looking back from this distance in time, it is horrific is it not? I have always asked, would a baker in Portsmouth really have wanted to kill a baker in Berlin? Would a butcher in the city really have wanted to kill a butcher in Tokyo?

Of course not. I am sure they would have preferred to have talked to them and learnt their way of doing things in their own trades.

Of course, it is despots and governments that cause wars and I am sure most civilian populations the world over would rather talk talk than war war.

Most of the photographs in this book were taken by *Evening News* photographer Victor Stewart who bravely went out in the midst of the carnage to record the scenes.

His collection of glass plates were kept at his home on Portsdown Hill.

Throughout the war, the *Evening News* never missed a day's publication. There were one or two near misses though the with drill hall across the road from the offices in Stanhope Road receiving a direct hit and another behind them in Victoria Park. I am grateful and thankful to Mark Waldron, the editor the *News* and the directors of Johnston Press for allowing me to use the photographs so as to record the modern locations today.

I must also thank Anthony Triggs, a former journalist and employee of the *News* for allowing me the use photographs from his book *Portsmouth – A Shattered City*. This is a book recording the scenes after much of the devastation had been cleared away and tidied up ready for the rebuilding of the city. Mind you, I can still remember a large bomb crater on the corner of Green Road and Elm Grove, Southsea as late as 1969.

I must thank my daughter Ursula for reading through the copy and her working with me to get files prepared for Halsgrove. I must also thank my wife, Audrey, who chauffeured me around the city with much criticism of her driving when she missed a corner of some side street I wanted her to turn down.

I dedicate this book to all of those lost, maimed and injured and who persevered in the 5 years of carnage that overtook the twentieth century.

Although it is seventy years since the end of the war, many still live in the city and talked to me of their lives during this period.

God Bless You all.

On the night of 11 July, 1940, the phoney war came to an end when Portsmouth took its first Luftwaffe raid. Heinkel bomber pilots heading for the dockyard overshot their target and their bombs landed in the Kingston area of the city.

The war had arrived. Eighteen residents of the city were killed and 80 injured. The much patronised Blue Anchor Hotel at Kingston Cross was one of the iconic old buildings damaged beyond repair. The actual address was 2, London Road, Kingston making it the first of hundreds of houses and businesses leading up to Hilsea.

One of the victims on that night was Police Constable Stanley Charles Spooner aged twenty-eight. He was killed close by the hotel when cycling to work during the raid. He was one of nine men serving in the police force in various forms, City Police, Police Fire Brigade, War Reserve, Special Constables who lost their lives as a result of enemy action. After the war the hotel was demolished and rebuilt as a single floor public house keeping its name although no longer a hotel of course. It closed its doors in 2010. It was divided in two with the right-hand side becoming a takeaway. In 2013 a much smaller establishment reopened its doors catering once again for the residents and shoppers of the North End district of the city.

Here we see the Blue Anchor Hotel on the morning of 12 July, 1940 and the destruction bombing can do. Police officers, ARP wardens, civilians and even a bus conductor peruse the destroyed hotel. Photographer Vic Stewart would have been standing on the junction of London Road and Kingston Crescent.

The same scene in 2015. The rebuilt public house closed its doors in 2010. To the right is a takeaway.
To the left the smaller establishment that re-opened its doors in 2013.

The Blue Anchor Hotel looking north along London Road with Kingston Crescent on the left. In this photograph also by Vic Stewart we can see more devastation caused by the bombing with buildings either side of the hotel also destroyed. A soldier stands guard and at attention with the .303 rifle at the slope no doubt to deter looters. Amazingly the bus system kept working and a trolley bus on route 4A heads for Cosham. The white building to the rear of the bus was the National Provincial Bank.

The same scene in 2015 with the trolley buses long gone. The Blue Anchor is now just half its rebuilt size with a takeaway to its right. The building to the right has been demolished and rebuilt as flats. The drive between the takeaway and the new block leads to the pub car park. The three buildings to the north of the Blue Anchor all survive to this day with the former Provincial Bank operating as NatWest.

Looking north along Commercial Road at its junction with Stanhope Road on the left. Here we see a crater caused by a high explosive. Although there is still much to do civilians make their way past the site with no one bothering them. Tram lines (right) from a previous form of transport which ended in 1936 have erupted from beneath the tarmac. Ron Brewer tells me the men in overalls assisting in matters were from the General Construction Company, Royal Engineers. Behind the lorry carrying what looks like a tank of tar is Station Street. At that time it was a narrow roadway leading to the railway goods yard, fish markets and Durham Street.

Looking north along Commercial Road from outside the bank to the left and railway station to the right.

The same scene in 2015. The bus is where the lorry was parked in the previous photo. Since those days many of the buildings surrounding the area have been demolished including Judd's Bar, and the road widened. Station Street is now a main thoroughfare leading to Arundel Street. What was a minor crossroads from Stanhope Road across to Station Street has since become a major junction with a mini roundabout causing all types of problems for modern traffic. The former area with its bars, old fashioned railway station, central post office and *Evening News* offices is much missed by many especially the author. It had so much atmosphere in days past when hundreds of sailors could be seen walking across this part of Commercial Road heading for the naval barracks in Queen Street.

The same view today with a modern bus replacing the lorry in the road.

The former entrance to the Hippodrome after the bombing. The front steps remained in situ until the site was rebuilt in the 1980s.

This photo was taken on the morning of 11 January, 1941, and we see the southern end of Commercial Road. It is the morning after the night before when on 10 January a massive blitz on the city caused mass destruction. In the top left of the photo can be seen part of the advertising awning for the Hippodrome Theatre that took a direct hit completely destroying a fine palace of dreams. To the right are the Prudential Buildings which housed solicitors, insurance and chartered accountant firms.

The entrance to the Hippodrome Theatre some days after it was destroyed.

South end of Commercial Road on 11 January , 1941, the day after the Hippodrome Theatre was destroyed. Sailors help to clear the rubble. In the distance the Theatre Royal stands untouched.

Opposite: *The same view today. This part of Commercial Road is now called Guildhall Walk and is a tree lined boulevard.*

The same view today with this part of Commercial Road now called Guildhall Walk. Although during the day it is a pleasant enough thoroughfare with several drinking establishments at night it becomes the home of the night-clubbing students and other young people. The Theatre Royal closed its doors in the late 1960 reopening after refurbishment. A massive fire to the rear destroying the dressing rooms closed it again. It has recently had a re-build of the dressing rooms and there will once again be two live theatres in the city.

The Hippodrome was another story. It was demolished and the location remained a bomb site well into the 1980s. On 13 October, 1984, the great English born American comedian Bob Hope was to appear at the Guildhall. Workmen digging on the site of the Hippodrome discovered a massive 500lb German bomb and the whole of the area, including the Guildhall, became an exclusion zone. It was eventually defused by men of the Bomb Disposal Unit, Royal Engineers, Chatham, Kent. The name of the theatre lives on however with Hippodrome House a building of office suites occupying the site.

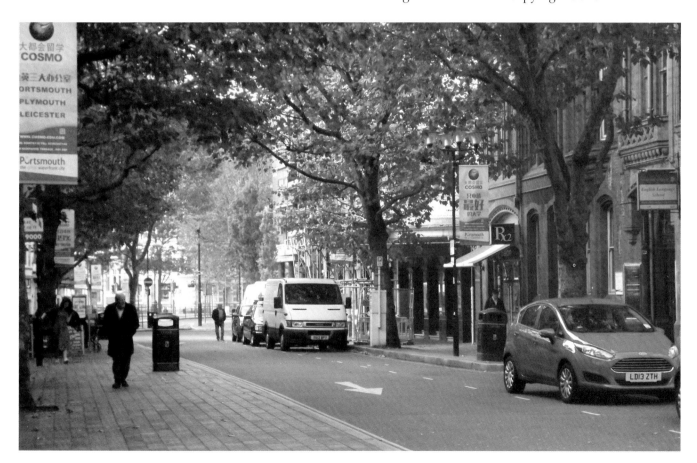

The corner of The Hard and Clock Street, Portsea on the morning of 23 December, 1940. To the right is the Ship Leopard.

In the picture on the opposite page we see the junction of The Hard and Clock Street on the morning of 23 December, 1940. It shows the carnage after a high explosive aimed at the dockyard whose main gate was just one hundred yards to the left of the picture. The mock Tudor building to the left is the Ship Anson which survived the bombing and still serves beers to this day.

The bomb landed on the Bedford and Chase public house located on The Hard at the junction with Clock Street. Six people were killed when they took shelter in the cellar of the pub. Two of those killed were mother and daughter Ivy and Barbara Burton aged forty-one and fifteen. Ivy and Barbara lived at 2, Clock Street and on the evening of 22 December, 1940, the air raid siren sounded and they both ran from the house to the pub and down into the cellar. Ivy had two sons who both remained in the house and sheltered under the stairs.

The pub took a direct hit, no doubt from a bomb aimed at the dockyard. The main gate was located just one-hundred yards from the pub. Four other residents were also killed in the cellar.

A fortnight later, Ivy's two sons were out and about when they came across an incendiary bomb. One of the sons, Alan, picked it up and carried it for a few yards when it exploded in his hands.

Alan was consumed in flames. Screaming in agony, he was taken to the Queen Alexandra Hospital at Cosham where he died of his injuries.

Strangely enough, he is not recorded under the term 'war dead' as it was basically an accident.

The following is a letter written by Barbara Burton to her Aunt Hilda just week before she was killed. The spelling and grammar are as written by Barbara:

15-12-40
Dear Auntie Hilda,
I am writing on behalf of Nanny and Mum. Nanny is very worried. Uncle Leonard is very ill indeed. Nanny said she don't know what to think of him.

Uncle Albert and Auntie Violet are living out in Denmead so they have taken him out there to live with them. I have come home for a couple of weeks to help Auntie Carrie in the shop. I should think you wouldn't come home for Christmas as it is terrible here. We are bombed practically every night. Last Thursday we thought our time had come as they dropped bombs all along the Hard. There are a good few shops down and houses damaged. St Mary's Road is terrible. There is not a single shop left standing and no traffic is allowed through. It has already been bombed three times.

Nanny received her parcel quite safe & also a letter. She told me to thank you very much indeed as it was just what she wanted, and Richard's photograph, well she is simply nuts about him. He is a lovely boy and nanny said he is the image of David

Aunt Rhoda is always talking about you and wondering how you all are. We have not seen much of her or the children for at least three-weeks and Auntie Rhoda didn't see Uncle Ernie very much as you know he is in the fire service and they don't get very much time off. Mummy sends her love & is sorry she cannot write as she has a lot to do. She cook for Nannie & Auntie Carrie & is very nervous about the raids. Last Thursday she fainted & didn't come round for ten minutes or more. The big guns have just boomed so I expect Wailing Winnie will be going soon and Nanny and Mummy are all on edge. Well Auntie Hilda there is not more to say as another gun has just fired and I want to get this letter finished tonight.

Auntie Gwennie is still at Denmead & Roy goes to school now. Auntie Gladys got a bit scared last week and went to Denmead with Auntie Gwennie. Doreen is not afraid of the raids. She goes to bed every night at the top of the house.

Nanny said she does not blame you for not coming home as it won't be much of a Christmas this year for anyone perhaps the New Year will bring forth better news.

Well I really must close now so cheerio hoping to hear from you soon.

> *With lots of love,*
> *From Barbara.*

P.S. Leonard sends a foreign note for Maurice & he will be writing soon to both of them.
> *For Richard*

XXXXXXX

Opposite: Here we see the same scene in 2015. The site of the Bedford and Chase has been replaced by an apartment block recently named Warrior House. The Ship Leopard and the Ship Anson survived the war and still serve to this day.

Below: Here we see mother and daughter Barbara (left) and Ivy Burton both killed when taking shelter in the cellar of the Bedford and Chase.

Barbara and Ivy Burton. Mother and daughter killed in the explosion.

The same view as on page 16 in 2015.

Here we see Locksway Road, Milton and some of the devastation brought upon the city by a V1 flying bomb during the final months of the war.

The house to the far right is No. 186 and belonged to the Atkin family. Mr Keith Atkin who was in the Anderson shelter to the rear of the house at the time tells me that when his mother returned to the house several items had been looted! The shop on the corner of Meryl Road was a grocers and a policeman can be seen guarding it against more looting.

We are at the junction with Meryl Road and the only item untouched is the post box standing erect on the corner as if to say, 'Come on then son, try and get me.'

The houses on either side of the junction have all been rebuilt to modern standards although the roof of the house to the right was being relaid on the day I took the photographs.

Most had thought that the bombing was all over until the menace of the V1 and V2 brought more death and destruction to cities all over the south of England and especially London.

Locksway Road, Milton at the junction with Meryl Road after the first V1 landed on the city.

I am glad to say that no V2 rockets dropped on the city.

I am also glad to say that there were no fatalities recorded after this incident.

In the modern photograph all is repaired and like new. The post box still stands guard on the corner of Meryl Road and a white van stands in place of the black van in the previous picture. Telephone wires have replaced the clear sky of 1944.

The same scene today. The post box remains.

This is a view looking down Unicorn Road from Market Way towards the Unicorn Gate, one of several gates into the dockyard. The sailors are posing with a maxim machine gun which has no ammunition belt attached. They are wearing the odd combination of gunnery gaiters and shoes rather than boots. The shelter behind the wall and above the post box was where the trains of the Dockyard Branch line used to pick up sailors when boarding troop trains.

The branch left the main line at Portsmouth & Southsea high level on a reserved line and ran in a reverse curve and crossed Edinburgh Road and Alfred Road where gates protected both. The line then entered the dockyard by a gate through the wall to the left of Unicorn Gate. The trees have their bases painted white for sighting in the blackout. To the right and out of camera is the close knit area of Duncan, Trafalgar, Nile, Abercrombie and Conway Streets. They were all decimated on the evening of 23 December, 1940.

A posed picture of sailors on the corner of Unicorn Road and Market Way. The maxim machine gun has no ammunition belt loaded and the sailors have the odd combination of gaiters and shoes rather than boots. Unicorn Gate can be seen in the distant right between the trees.

The modern photograph was taken from the same location but in a more dangerous position as it is now sited in the middle of a two lane dual carriageway taking heavy traffic in and out of the city. The original Unicorn Gate can again be seen in the distance on the right between the trees.

In recent years a large new wooden gate has been erected further south down Unicorn Road for security reasons. It has the red chevron on the left of it.

The trees are all new. The railway succumbed in the early 1970s and the wall was demolished. The track bed was brought into the public domain and planted with shrubs and trees.

To take the same photograph today is a very dangerous task. A two lane dual carriageway at the crossroads of Unicorn Road, Alfred Road and Market Way means non-stop traffic. The sailors would have been located where the keep left bollard is to front of camera. Unicorn Gate can be seen, again, between the trees in the distance.

Here we see three sailors and a Royal Marine giving some assistance to an elderly lady who had, perhaps, had her home hit. We can see a dustbin outside the front gate and a bus stop sign. To the rear of the removal lorry can be seen the lady's gas cooker.

It is a wet day in Jessie Road, Southsea at the junction of the crossroads with Talbot Road. Behind the sailor to the left holding the wooden bench is Wringle's the fishmonger and a face can be seen at the window watching events unfold.

The junction of Jessie Road and Talbot Road: here we see three sailors and a Royal Marine assisting an elderly lady remove items including this tin bath.

In the modern picture we can see that Mr Wringle has since retired and the shop has become a Chinese takeaway. The bus stop is still in the same location although a drop kerb now assists passengers in boarding. All the houses are the same, except for the modern double glazing of course.

The same scene in 2015. Mr Wringle's fish shop is now a takeaway. The bus stop remains although a drop kerb assists passengers in boarding.

The Territorial Army Drill Hall in Stanhope Road was built in 1901 to the plans of architect A. Bone. It was destroyed on the night of 10/11 January, 1941, and remained a wreck until after the war when it was rebuilt. The former battlement-like tower on the south west corner of the roof was taken down and a plain roof installed taking away much of the building's presence. The TA gave the building up in the 1990s and it was converted to a nightclub called Liquid & Envy.

The Grade 2 listed two-storey building is all that remains along Stanhope Road which once housed the Central Post Office with sorting offices. It was busy day and night with bags of mail taken across the road to mail trains waiting in the platforms of Portsmouth & Southsea Station.

On the left of the picture can be seen part of the offices of the *Portsmouth Evening News* which, apart from a few broken windows, remained untouched throughout the war. The paper never failed to produce an edition over the 5 years of conflict.

Opposite page: The same view today with the reconstructed roof line and conversion to a nightclub. The *Evening News* moved out of town to new offices at Hilsea in 1969 and a towering plate-glass structure for Zurich Insurance was built on the site, completed in 1973. They have since moved on and after remaining empty for many years it is to be a hotel, private flats and student accommodation.

Here we see the Connaught Drill Hall in Stanhope Road after taking a direct hit. To the left can be seen part of the Evening News offices.

The hall was rebuilt after the war and is now a Grade 2 listed building. It became a night club around 2005.

In this dramatic photograph of Commercial Road at its junction with Edinburgh Road we see firemen attack a blaze that is burning in rooms above the Milk Bar café. The stools from the café line the pavement outside. Hoses are also being played through the window of the Halifax Building Society. Hose pipes litter the streets and firemen, clad in leathers and steel helmets on the right, remove a ladder from their appliances. Just out of sight around the bend to the left is the Central Hotel which also went up in flames. In the distance can be seen Barclays Bank shrouded in smoke with the very popular Swiss Café to its left.

Opposite page: The same location in 2015. The Halifax has since disappeared and the premises are up to let. In the distance, Barclays Bank still trades. The Swiss Café has long since gone and the building demolished. The new building houses Pearl Insurance. Where firemen once fought the fires, bus shelters line the much-widened pavement. I wonder if the gentleman sitting in the shelter knew such dramatic events occurred behind where he is sitting?

The corner of Commercial Road and Edinburgh Road. Firemen fight fire in rooms above the Milk Bar café. In the distance is Barclays Bank and to the left of it the Swiss Café.

All peaceful in Commercial Road although the Halifax has departed and the building is up for let. In the distance, Barclays Bank still trades although the Swiss Café has long gone, the building since demolished and now home to Pearl Insurance.

Here we see Highbury Buildings, Portsmouth Road, Cosham on the morning after the night before 6 December, 1940. One of four 250Kg bombs landed on the shopping parade killing Joan Millet who lived around the corner in Chatsworth Avenue and Frederick Walron who lived in Park Grove. Some five months later when the debris was being cleared the remains of a sailor were also found. It appears he had dived into the front door of one of the shops and the building came down on top of him.

Opposite page: The same scene in 2015. The central part of Highbury Buildings has been repaired and it looks like nothing had ever occurred on the site.

Highbury Buildings, Portsmouth Road, Cosham 6 December, 1940.

Highbury Buildings renewed 2015.

Here we see what remained of the Carlton Cinema in High Street, Cosham on the morning of 6 December, 1940. A luxurious palace of dreams, the cinema had a large attendance on the evening of 5 December including the Lady Mayoress. She left just before the cinema was hit by one of four 250Kg that landed that evening. Unfortunately, although many were injured, three young lads were killed. Samuel Bannister aged eighteen, Derek Jones aged seventeen and Sidney Pearce aged eighteen. The cinema was rebuilt and opened again while the war still raged. It was later called the Classic, Essoldo, Cannon, ABC, Reeltime and lastly Cineplex.

The former Carlton Cinema, High Street, Cosham after the night of 5 December, 1940.

The cinema closed its doors for the last time on 1 November, 2007. It stood vacant for several years but was finally demolished in December 2010. Apartments and offices now stand on the site.

Site of the Carlton, later named the Essoldo among many others, in 2015. It was demolished in 2010.

We are looking west down Queen Street with the Royal Naval Barracks, HMS Victory on the right after the premises took a hit in March 1941. I believe this photograph was taken on the morning of 11 March, 1941 when, on the previous night, one of the fourteen direct hits suffered by the barracks was a bomb on the parade ground shelters near the Main Gate. Seven ratings were killed. The damaged building on the right looks like it could be the structure that the sailors were sheltering in. Many sailors can be seen in the street outside the Main Gate which is behind the lamp standard, centre photo. In the distance is the Royal Naval Arms public house which was demolished in 1972. Attached to the railings can be seen corrugated sheeting which denied passers-by looking onto the parade ground.

After this incident the editor of the *Portsmouth Evening News* wrote to the Admiralty asking if the sheets could be taken down on a permanent basis. It was agreed to and thereafter civilians could be spectators when the Royal Marine band played at divisions and other parade ground activities. It has since been built on.

The Royal Naval Barracks, HMS Victory, Queen Street, Portsea 1941.

The Royal Naval Barracks now renamed HMS Nelson 2015.

The modern image shows the same scene today with the brick wall and railings back in situ. Since that time Queen Street has altered behind camera with a large junction and the road widened. The Main Gate is still in situ but not used as a traffic entrance into the barracks although there are gates if required. Part of the wall and railings either side have been removed and the gate stands in its own ground enabling taxis to treat it as a roundabout and drop off without entering the barracks as such.

The Royal Naval Arms has long since gone and the wall to the far side of the Main Gate demolished and a lawned area laid. The majority of the old barrack block and all other buildings seen in the photograph have since been demolished and new buildings built to modern standards.

Here we see the scene looking from the wardroom across Queen Street into the Royal Naval Barracks parade ground.

The wall of the barracks has been totally destroyed. Just to the right can be seen the catholic cathedral.

The Royal Naval Barracks, Queen Street after the raid of 12 August, 1940. The Roman Catholic Cathedral can be seen behind the tree on the right.

Below is the same view today. The barracks' wall although repaired, had to be partly demolished at its east end and rebuilt into a sharper curve for road widening purposes in the 1970s. The Roman Catholic Cathedral can be seen in full, the tree in the previous photo having been felled.

The same scene today. The Roman Catholic Cathedral in Edinburgh Road can be seen on the right.

Set up beside the Cenotaph alongside the Guildhall here we see a street canteen to supplement emergency arrangements and minister to people's needs. The posts of the canteen have been anchored in old tea chests. Up on the embankment an up train overlooks the site. To the right of the top of the canteen can be seen one of the two stone machine gunners who guard the Cenotaph. Many of the people seen are not carrying their gas masks it seems, so it may have been in the early days of the war before a gas attacked threatened.

Opposite page: The same scene today with cars and vans displacing the cycle and canteen. A modern train overlooks the scene and the machine gunner still stands guard at the entrance to the Cenotaph with his comrade with bandages around his head seen above the roof of the van.

A street canteen set up beside the Cenotaph alongside the Guildhall.

The same scene today with cars and vans in place of the canteen and people enjoying a cup of tea.

On the morning of 23 December, 1940, a customer entered Clark's general store on the corner of St James' Road and Brougham Road, Southsea.

He made his purchases and offered a five-pound note to pay for it. Unfortunately there was not enough change in the till and so one of the shop girls, Joyce Penfold offered to run across St James' Road to her father's butcher's shop to ask him to change up the five pound note. It cost her life. The store was owned by Mr George Clark and his wife Beatrice, thus Clark's Corner. It was a very popular place to shop as it was one of those places that sold everything.

Mr Clark agreed to Joyce running across the road to get the change and as she did so the siren sounded. Her father, George, changed the note and said to Joyce 'You had better get in the shelter in the back yard.' She said: 'I'll just run this change back to the shop and I'll come back to you.' She never did. As she entered the shop it took a direct hit from a high explosive completely destroying the building and killing all inside. George Penfold who was waiting at the door of his butcher's for his daughter's return was blasted through his shop out into the back yard but survived. George was shocked and shaken but came to his senses and ran across the road with an ARP warden and entered Pugsley's wine merchants (seen on the left of the original photograph) and ran down into the cellar. George thought that his daughter might have been in the adjoining cellar and obtaining an axe knocked down an adjoining wall but to no avail.

After making a search of the wreckage there was no sign of Joyce and George, along with his son Dan, made their way to the family home at 3, Lower Farlington Road, Farlington where George broke the news to his wife Daisy that their lovely daughter had been taken.

Joyce Penfold.

The morning of 23 December, 1940 and we see Clark's Corner after being hit earlier that day.

Another daughter Irene, aged twenty at the time, said that her father's face was blackened and streaked with tears he had cried for his beloved daughter.

Daisy Penfold later made her way to the scene and remained on site using accommodation above the butcher's shop.

It was not until two days later that Joyce's body was found. Joyce was still wearing a bracelet she had always worn and George showed it to his wife to confirm the remains were of Joyce. She was interred in Highland Road Cemetery.

In the centre of the original photograph, the back of a man in a white shirt and black trousers can be seen to the left of the man facing camera. That is George Penfold searching for his daughter.

The others who were killed that day were Mr and Mrs Clark, Lilian Barton aged twenty-seven, Charles Payne aged fifteen, Kathleen Paine aged twenty-four, and Thomas Pinnock aged sixteen.

I have been able to obtain a photograph of Joyce loaned by Bonnie Comlay who is the granddaughter of George Penfold. Joyce would have been her aunt had she lived.

The same scene today. A few houses from the period remain in Brougham Road.

On 16 August, 1943, death and destruction came to Fifth Street, Buckland. To prove bombing makes no distinction between young or old it took Alma Marks aged fifty-three along with her grandchildren Patricia seven and Valerie four months. Grace Ripiner aged thirty-five was also taken along with her daughter Lana aged twelve months.

In the photograph we are looking north along Fifth Street from St Mary's Road and in the photograph is a little girl with white socks. She is Mrs Jean Phillip née Foley. In the pram as a baby is Mrs Pamela Mockford nee Mannell.

Jean told that the previous evening the family had made their way to the tunnels in Portsdown Hill and had returned to their home at 94, Clive Road, Fratton. Her mother heard that Fifth Street had been hit. She said to Jean that she would have to go and find out if her niece was all well.

On arrival they found devastation all around with many of the houses at the St Mary's Road end of the street completely destroyed and others seriously damaged and uninhabitable. Luckily all of Jean's family survived. In the photo from left to right we see: Lottie Mockford, Lottie

Looking down Fifth Street on the morning of 17 August, 1943.

Foley (Jean's mother), Jean in white socks, in the pram is baby Pamela Mannel, and Ada Pauley an aunt. The table on the left with the barley sugar legs belongs to Pamela's parents. Many years later when the family lived in Cuthbert Road and the first television was brought into the house it stood on that table. Out of sight up the stairs in the house on the left would be Pamela's father, Reginald who was doing his best to sort out the family's possessions. This was the second time the family had been hit as a few months earlier they had been bombed out of Shearer Road.

The modern photograph shows the same scene today. All the houses on the right seen in the previous photo have been demolished as far down as the houses with the bay windows.

All the houses on the left have been demolished and replaced with modern housing set back from the road.

The same location in 2015. All the houses on the right of the former photo have been demolished down to the houses with bay windows

Looking down Prince George Street, Portsea towards Cross Street with Brickwoods brewery hidden in the smoke. The burning tower belonged to St John the Evangelist church. Dating from 1789 this was another of Portsmouth's many churches that went up in flames on 10/11 January, 1941. The fire service and wardens fought valiantly to save the building but in vain. The complete tower was made of wood.

Opposite page: The same scene today. Admiralty Tower, a recent residential block built on part of the site of the former brewery, overlooks the location of the former church.

Here we see what was the magnificent church St John the Evangelist in Prince George Street, Portsea.

The same scene today with the former church site now overlooked by a modern tower block, Admiralty Building.

This is St Alban's church, Copnor Road although the photograph was taken from Coniston Avenue. A lone Stuka approached the railway line alongside the city airport and gas works but dropped its bomb too early. It landed in the centre of the church doing the damage seen. There was, fortunately, no loss of life but 27 people were injured. The pilot never lived to see the error of his ways as he was shot down soon after, losing his life. Apart from the damage to the church the houses in Coniston Avenue have all been damaged by the blast. Search out the furthest garden from camera and you will see the upturned remains of a saloon car.

St Alban's church, Copnor seen from Coniston Avenue after a lone Stuka dropped its load aiming for the railway, and blew out the centre of the church.

Below we see St Alban's church and houses rebuilt. If you look closely at the church in wet weather the line where the old brickwork finishes and the new starts can be easily seen. In this view it can be seen between the fourth and fifth windows from the right.

The end house has been extended with a garage under the first floor.

The same scene today with all the houses on the left now in good repair. In damp weather a line can be seen separating the old brick from the new on the church between the fifth and sixth windows from the right.

Here we see St Alban's church from the Copnor Road side. The damage caused by just one bomb was massive. Perhaps it was fortunate that the pilot had misjudged his target and failed to hit anything nearer the gas works – otherwise the outcome could have been devastating.

St Albans church, Copnor from Copnor Road. The excessive damage caused by a single bomb can be seen.

Rebuilt and as good as new.

Even during the war with the shortage of fuel people still had to get about. Here we see two naval officers with a rating in the rear in a smart pony and trap.

They are passing the Grenada pub on the corner of Waverley Road heading west. Behind the officers would be the remains of the former Southsea branch line terminus station. The soldier has no worry about being knocked off his cycle in the traffic-free roads of the time.

Opposite: The same scene today and what a difference. The once grand Granada public house was closed many years ago to become the nightclub Harry Limes. That also closed in time and it is now The Lounge.

The former railway station site remained vacant for many, many years until housing was built.

The Victorian houses in the distance have altered little over the years.

Although there was a war on people still had to get about. Two officers use a smart pony and trap turn-out.

The naval officers have long gone and so has the once superb Granada pub. It is now a nightclub.

The houses seen are the backs of houses in Locksway Road at the junction with Milton Road. This must have been indiscriminate bombing as there were no naval or military installations in this area of close-knit housing and parks. Two ARP men can be seen to the far left searching through the rubble. What could be a council worker's bicycle is parked on the kerb and he is digging a hole to the left of it?

The premises look to have been a former clothier, if the sign to the left is anything to go by, as it tells us it sold Swallow raincoats with the slogan Fine In The Rain.

Here we see the back of the houses in Locksway Road at the junction with Milton Road.

The same scene today with much building work now covering the former location.

The barber's shop named Sid's was well known as many of the Portsmouth Football Club players of the 1948/49 and 1949/50 Double winning team had their hair cut by Sid. He has since retired.

The two small windows of the house in Locksway Road remain although now double-glazed. The chimney pots also remain although no doubt redundant with modern heating systems.

The black and white kerbstones have also long been replaced.

The same scene today with the wreckage now built over and a barber's and ladies' hairdressers on the site.

Here we see what happened to the front of two fine houses at the end of the terrace in Locksway Road at the junction of Milton Road.

So badly damaged were they that they were demolished. Local residents pose for the camera with no apparent care in the world. Cycles rule on the pavement.

Locksway Road and Milton Road junction. The two end houses had to be demolished they were so badly damaged.

Today we see the same houses as in the then shot but the two end houses have now long gone. A row of shops was built on the site.

Modern cars again ruin the shot, taking the place of the cycles. A large lorry was parked just out of sight from this cropped shot, which prevented a closer view of the scene.

Locksway Road and Milton Road junction today. The two former end houses were demolished and shops built on the site.

This is the scene of devastation in April 1941 after Commercial Road took a hit form the Luftwaffe. We are looking south towards the Guildhall.

To the right was McIlroy's department store and as we can see completely gutted by the firestorm. Between the store and the next building down was Thomas Street now no longer with us. Although a dangerous situation existed, local people were still allowed to pass within a few yards of the building. The road is covered in debris but the girls with their cycles and the soldier smoking a cigarette are more concerned with having their picture taken than stepping on glass. Take notice of the white building to the far left with the chimneys above and Surrey Kent emblazoned on the wall.

Believe it or not, this is the same scene today and it took me a devil of a time to locate it. I walked up and down Commercial Road looking for some sign of anything remaining and it was not until I reached the northern end of the road and looked back from Market Way roundabout did I see, among the trees and street furniture which litters the roundabout, the Surrey Kent white building mentioned earlier, in the distance. I always feel elated when this happens. I had to stand on the roundabout to get the shot as McIlroy's site is now part of it. The Soldier seen would be where the black and white chevron on the edge of the roundabout is now and the girls with their cycles on the lush grass. To the right of the roundabout is Market Way leading to Southsea and the exit to the left leads to Lake Road.

McIlroy's scene today. The white building to the left in the former picture is the same building to the left in the modern picture.

Opposite page: *Looking south along Commercial Road and we see the former and very popular McIlroy's store on the immediate right. Take note of the white building to the far left of the picture.*

The massive five-story building to the left was once the Royal Sailors' Rest off Chandos and Buckingham Streets, Landport. Miss Agnes Weston built the Rest in 1882 'For the Glory of God and the Good of the Service.' Thousands of naval men found comfort and safety at the Rest. After having spent months at sea sleeping in hammocks and sharing washing facilities to have a room of their own must have been a delight. Some years after the war the Sailors' Rest opened up once again on the corner of Edinburgh Road and Unicorn Road.

The massive five-story building to the left was once the Royal Sailors' Rest, off Chandos and Buckingham Streets, Landport. Miss Agnes Weston built the Rest in 1882.

The same scene today looking up Chandos Street from Commercial Road. All around the streets have been pedestrianised.

It is possible that the building occupied by Boots on the right-hand side is a survivor from the war, albeit refurbished.

The same scene today looking up Chandos Street from Commercial Road. All around the streets have been pedestrianised. I am not sure if the building to the right is the same refurbished structure in the former photograph – possibly. In the distance Tesco reigns supreme.

All that remains of C&A and the LDB (Landport Drapery Bazaar) on the morning of 11 January, 1941. In the distance are the smouldering remains of the Timothy Whites Depository. Timothy White started the company in Portsmouth in 1848 and in 1935 merged with Taylor's Drugs Company to form the popular Timothy White and Taylors. Former City Police Fireman Eddie Wallace was one of the crew who fought this fire and he told me;

'At 8 p.m. with my colleagues, I was inside the Landport Drapery Bazaar and we were successful in putting out a fire on the top floor caused by an incendiary. We then transferred our actions to the top floor of the big Depository of Timothy White and Taylors in Buckingham Street. We put that fire out and gazed for a very short while from the roof at the scene around us. It seemed we were in the centre of Dante's Inferno!

The gutted remains of C&A, Commercial Road opposite Edinburgh Road junction, and LDB on the corner of Arundel Street and Commercial Road. 11 January, 1941.

'Whilst there a large HE (high explosive) landed on Landports and it seemed as if the whole building exploded – so much for our earlier efforts. We took our engine back into Commercial Road only to learn that this second raid had hit the water mains in Old Portsmouth and also somewhere in Buckland and so there was no water for several hours until the "powers that be " got a supply of water going from the bottom of Broad Street and the Canoe Lake and Flathouse.'

Arundel Street can be just seen past the wreckage. C&A never opened up on the same site after the war but a new store was built some 500 yards further north in Commercial Road.

The LDB took over the whole corner and became very popular. It is now a branch of Debenhams. The whole of this area including the first quarter mile of Arundel Street has been pedestrianised.

The glass-plated building of Debenhams replaces the burnt out remains of the former stores that once occupied this space.

This is a view looking west down High Street, Old Portsmouth after the bombers passed. They opened up a vista never seen before when all the three-storey shops that once lined the High Street in front of the cathedral were destroyed opening a view of the south side of the cathedral hardly seen before.

What remained of the buildings were demolished after the war and a lawn laid in their place. In the road a former transport system in the form of tram lines still lie in the road ten years after their demise and trolley bus wires hang loose overhead in their place.

Looking west down High Street, Old Portsmouth. How the Anglican Cathedral was missed by the bombers must be a miracle.

Today the houses and shops have all gone and the lawn laid and trees planted giving a countrified view of the cathedral. Trayler's, on the corner of Lombard Road, ceased to exist and a modern block of apartments has been built on the site.

A memorial to several people killed in a sweetshop on the corner of Lombard Road can be seen on the corner of the former churchyard.

The same scene in 2015 and all is new apart from the cathedral.

In this scene we are looking north along Green Road, Southsea from its junction with Elm Grove. The bottom right hand corner would lead into Belmont Street.

In a way that would be impossible in today's PC world the men have attached a rope to an unsafe wall and are preparing to bring it down. Demolition in its most simplistic form. Beyond the wall which is about to come down are some houses with dormer windows in the roof.

Looking along Green Road, Southsea as men of the Pioneer Corps bring down a dangerous wall.

In this same view today most of what was seen in the earlier view has gone apart from the houses with the dormer windows which still stand guard along this quiet residential area of Southsea. In the distance a modern high-rise block of flats overlooks the scene. Cottage Grove is the right-hand turning in the distance.

Looking along Green Road, Southsea 2015.

In this somewhat horrendous scene we are looking at what was one of the finest stores in Southsea, Handley's. It stood on the corner (thus Handley's Corner) of the northern end of Palmerston Road and the junction with Osborne Road. It was part of the highly affluent shopping areas of Southsea.

It is the morning of 11 January, 1941, after the firestorm hit Portsmouth the night before. Although there is much danger all around civilians, like the lady walking across the front of the burnt-out store, seem to be taking it in their stride. Hoses litter the roadway and the man to the far left looks absolutely shattered after, perhaps, being on duty the whole night through.

Horrendous scenes on the morning of 11 January, 1941. This is Handley's Corner at the junction of Palmerston Road and Osborne Road.

Handley's Corner 2015. After remaining vacant land for several years Palmerston Road was rebuilt and Handley's new store can be seen in the same location.

It later became a Debenhams. Although the area has lost some of its influence as a top shopping area, the houses around still remain the property of the affluent.

Where the men of the Pioneer Corps are clearing rubble from the street taxis now ply their trade whilst the northern side of Palmerston Road has now been pedestrianised.

Handley's rebuilt their store after the war but it has since been taken over by Debenhams.

Stanley Street, Southsea after the Luftwaffe had passed in the pretence of bombing naval and military installations. Even with their backs to us the men of the Pioneer Corps seem bewildered at what they are facing. Apart from the danger of bombing and the shrapnel from the exploding shells, another danger is quite obvious: wood splinters. Imaging splinters of wood travelling through the air at great speed and the damage they would do to a human body. Frightening.

Stanley Street before its junction with Palmerston Road. The danger from splintered wood can be seen.

All is clear in this same scene photograph. To the right a branch of the John Lewis company Knight & Lees have built new premises, bringing back a little up-market shopping to an area that was supreme in shopping in this affluent area of Southsea before the war.

Stanley Street 2015. The street is now a cul-de-sac since Palmerston Road was pedestrianised.

This is the scene in Lake Road, Landport, Portsmouth on 24 August, 1940 after the Princes Theatre had a bomb through its roof. It was a Saturday afternoon during a children's matinee. This fine theatre which was converted to a cinema in 1924 and with a frontage not unlike the New Theatre Royal was decimated along with the Baptist church to the right of photograph. Of the many children in the theatre at the time and reports of several casualties in my researches, it appears that there was just one fatality. He was a Mr Harry White age twenty-six who lived at 66, High Street, Old Portsmouth.

To the left of the theatre is the Sultan pub on the corner of Alexandra Road which survived the raid.

The Princes Theatre, Lake Road on the morning of 24 August, 1940. Imagine sitting in a theatre and a bomb exploding in the roof above you?

The location of the Princes Theatre 2015. Several blocks of flats including Blendworth House have been built on the site.

The same scene today with the theatre, church and pub all long since gone. Several blocks of flats now stand on the site of the Princes and with the passing of time no one will ever know that such a magnificent theatre stood on this site.

This is the scene soon after a bomb landed between 42 and 44 Sunningdale Road, Copnor on 10 November, 1940. This was the home of Mr and Mrs Pearce whose son Laurence had married just five weeks before.

He and his young wife Iris lived with an aunt, and on this afternoon they were visiting his parents at number 42, when a lone raider released his cargo of death. The explosive landed between the two houses killing Laurence, Iris and a Mr Alfred Purkis who lived next door at number 44. The couple were buried alongside one another in Kingston cemetery Iris in her wedding dress she had worn just five weeks previously.

42 and 44 Sunningdale Avenue, Copnor, Portsmouth after a raid on 10 November, 1940.

Laurence and Iris Pearce on their wedding day. They were killed five weeks later.

The same two houses today.

On the evening of 23 December, 1940, the residents of Conway Street and all the close knit neighbouring streets were, no doubt, preparing for a frugal Christmas. There are several theories to what actually occurred. One is that a German bomber loaded with high explosives to secure serious damage to the dockyard released its bomb too early causing it to explode in the Conway Street area.

Another theory is that the bomber was brought down by gunfire and crashed with its load within the same street. There is no evidence that any wreckage of the aeroplane was ever found amid the carnage that remained after the HE landed. At least fourteen people died but there may have been more who were obliterated in the explosion. It was not to be a happy Christmas in that part of Portsmouth that year.

Conway Street to the north of Charlotte Street ran parallel with Unicorn Road. Abercrombie, Nile and Trafalgar Streets ran between the two of them.

All of the named streets were later demolished and whereas at one time they all stood outside of the dockyard wall to the south of Unicorn Gate, the whole area is now within the former dockyard, now Portsmouth Naval Base. The Unicorn Gate entrance has been moved 500 yards south and the Conway Street area is now a car and lorry park for naval base vehicles. Unicorn Gate itself has since had part of the adjoining dockyard wall demolished and is now in the middle of a roundabout.

On 23 December, 1940, a massive explosion outside the dockyard walls caused devastation to the Conway Street area. Here is a street scene.

This is part of the massive crater caused by whatever it was that destroyed Conway Street and adjoining streets.

Roughly the same scene today – a car park in an area within the former dockyard (now naval base) wall.

On the night of 24 August, 1940, the raiders again visited Portsmouth and again many civilians had to suffer the onslaught. Several high explosives landed along St Mary's Road and destroyed much of the housing at the junction with Shearer Road.

On the evening of 23 August, 1940, Stoker James Hoad and his wife Ethel were visiting friends at 29, St Mary's Road, Kingston. Also present were Ethel's sister Winifred, her husband Frank, along with David Erwin, Ethel's father. Also in the house was James and Ethel's six-week-old baby Pamela. When the siren sounded they all ran to the Anderson shelter in the back garden and waited. Soon after the bombing began and soon after that the shelter took a direct hit. All but one within were killed. When the rescue squads arrived they began to take the bodies away and found Ethel lying face down, dead. As they turned her gently over they found wrapped within her coat her baby Pamela. She was critically ill but alive. The poor mite was rushed to hospital where her injuries were assessed. She had a fractured femur, abrasions to her legs and head – but one injury was no scratch. A piece of shrapnel had entered her left thigh and left a terrible scar. Over the years, as Pamela grew, so did the scar giving her a legacy from the war.

The junction of Shearer Road and St Mary's Road, 25 August, 1940. All the houses in the distance had to be demolished.

The same junction today. Shearer Road junction and the pavement has been made narrower for safer crossing of what is now a one way street coming out of the road.

There is a further sad twist to this story in that James's father Chief Petty Officer Frank Edwin Hoad was serving in the Navy at Portland, Dorset. When the news came through that his son and daughter-in-law had been killed in the air raid and his granddaughter might have been a casualty as well, he took a pistol and shot himself. The deputy coroner brought in a verdict of suicide whilst the balance of his mind was disturbed. Another casualty of the war, albeit by his own hand, but ultimately a victim of events that he could not have anything to do with.

Opposite page: The junction of St Mary's Road and Shearer Road on the morning of 25 August, 1940. Brick rubble and timber along with a fallen telegraph pole litter the streets. Again we see civilians walking past the scene with an air of 'you will not stop me getting to where I want to be.'

Above: All the houses seen in the previous photo have been demolished and new houses and a Baptist Church erected in their place. Shearer Road has been made narrower making it safer for pedestrians to cross this now one way street. A lot safer than on the evening of 25 August, 1940 anyway.

In these two photographs we see the Bishop's House attached to the Roman Catholic Cathedral in Edinburgh Road, Portsmouth.

High explosive bombs did the damage, destroying not only the building but the magnificent theological library which included many priceless old manuscripts and first editions. Luckily some early printed books were recovered from the cellar.

There was also loss of life. Three domestic staff were killed in the raid. Maud Bushell and sisters Mary and

This is all that remained of the Bishop's House attached to the Roman Catholic Cathedral in Edinburgh Road, Portsmouth.

Bridget Linnane from Coopers Park, County Clare, Eire were the three innocent ladies taken after the house fell in on them.

The Bishop's House was reduced to just a heap of rubble and waste. The cathedral itself was built of local red bricks from Fareham and was opened in 1882. It was the first cathedral built in the city, the Anglican building in Old Portsmouth formerly being a church. The main body of the cathedral survived the bombing.

The Bishop's house was restored in 1950, and today looks as good as new.

Where the rubble lay in Edinburgh Road modern cars now park up alongside a restored Bishop's House.

On the evening of 15 July, 1944, most people had gone to bed thinking that the war was almost over. Almost. Two V1 flying bombs landed on the city, one in Locksway Road and the other here between Winstanley Road and Newcomen Road, Stamshaw. This one did the most damage killing at least 25 residents including four of one family, the Channons, and injuring many more. In the photograph many workmen can be seen trying to clear the destruction on the following morning. Notice in the middle of the photograph a man placing a large radio on to a pram with a young lad looking at the camera.

Looking east up Newcomen Road, Stamshaw, Portsmouth on the morning of 16 July, 1944, after a V1 hit this part of town.

Looking east up Newcomen and much of the housing on the left is new. Modern repairs are taking place on buildings that replaced those destroyed.

In the old image, we are looking east along Newcomen Road from the Portsmouth Harbour foreshore end of the road. The damage sustained would suggest a larger loss of life than what actually occurred.

In the 2015 equivalent, the new houses that replaced the blitzed buildings of 1944 on the left are under repair. I wonder if they will last as long as the solid brick-built turn of the last century houses they replaced and others that remain further along the road.

The Big Clear Up

At war's end the city of Portsmouth had lost 6625 properties with 6549 seriously damaged and 68,886 in need of repair. Eight schools were destroyed with 20 damaged. One hospital, four cinemas and a music hall were also destroyed. Thankfully Pompey, known for a pub on every corner, could suffer the damage to licensed premises as 61 public houses, 49 beer houses and 40 off-licences ceased to operate.

Most of the damage from the blitz was suffered in the south-western corner of the island, (for those reading this not from Portsmouth, it is actually Portsea Island) with bombers aiming for the dockyard. Other parts of the city blitzed were the Kings Road, Palmerston Road and Commercial Road, all high street shopping areas with many large company stores going up in flames.

Just under 1000 people were killed not including service-men who did not count under the civilian lost total.

Considering those lost when the Royal Naval Barracks shelters were hit and those on leave I should think the total killed over the six years of war was over a thousand.

Many of the following photographs come from Anthony Triggs book *Portsmouth – A Shattered City* and most were taken in the two years after the war's end.

Much is unrecognisable as to what was there before and I have had to search for the remaining buildings hidden in today's modern housing and blocks of flats.

As I said previously, the biggest problem today is traffic. I sometimes visited a photographic location three or four times to take a 'now' photo. In the end I often had to take the shot with the van/lorry in shot.

I am thankful to Tony Triggs for allowing me the privilege of using his photographs for this part of the book.

The junction of St George's Square and Ordnance Row, Portsea. Totterdell's Hotel now closed for business.

Opposite page: This was Totterdell's Family Hotel located at the junction of St George's Square and Ordnance Row, Portsea. After a century it ceased business when it was destroyed by the Luftwaffe. To the far right can be seen the Eagle Tavern and the brick building, with SWS (Static Water Supply) emblazoned on its wall, was a communal bomb shelter. To the distant left the road leads on to the Hard. Beyond the trees is the Odeon-style Southern Railway signal box still in use at that time. Tram lines, not used since 1936, still line the street.

Below: After Totterdell's Hotel was demolished the local firm of Linnington's car dealers had a garage built on the site. This has since been demolished and a memorial to Isambard Kingdom Brunel, the constructor of much of the Great Western Railway and ship designer, is located on the site. Brunel was born locally in Britain Street in 1806. The Eagle pub has been converted into a home. The signal box is still standing but long since taken out of use. The tram lines may have been lifted but perhaps still lie under inches of tarmac like in many parts of Portsmouth to this day.

The same scene today. For many years Linnington's Garage was located on the site of the former hotel. It is now home to the Isambard Kingdom Brunel memorial. He was born locally in 1806.

Looking up Queen Street, Portsea from the dockyard main gate now called Victory Gate with dockyard wall to the left. Not a lot to reveal in the way of damage to buildings but more of interest is the car to the right with the very large TAXI written on a board and attached to the car's bumper. The two sailors in the street are wearing the three-quarter length greatcoats issued then and for many years after. It was not unusual to see them with unofficial white scarves being worn. To the left can be seen two sailors pushing a cart.

Looking along Queen Street from the junction with the Hard. The dockyard wall is to the left.

The same view up Queen Street today.

The same view today with the cars and taxi long gone. It is rare to see a sailor in uniform as well. The former Main Gate into the dockyard to the left of camera is now called Victory Gate. It is no longer a main entrance to what is now the naval base.

Looking north along a decimated Clarence Street, Landport, Portsmouth after the wreckage of war had been cleared away. In the distance can be seen the chimney of the boiler house to St Mary's Hospital. To the distant left is the Royal Navy Pitt Street baths.

Believe it or not but this photo was taken from the exact same location as the modern shot opposite. What remains of Clarence Street lies beyond the trees in the centre of the photograph. The cars in the forefront are where the Tricorn shopping centre and multi-storey car park once stood. Built and opened in 1966 it survived for twenty-five years before being demolished.

Behind camera is Charlotte Street, a once thriving local market which has all but disappeared. A few stalls now appear in Commercial Road but nothing like the once popular area of Charlotte Street.

This is all that remains of Clarence Street, Landport, Portsmouth after the clearing up of rubble and demolishing damaged buildings.

Taken from the same point as the previous photograph, the remains of Clarence Street are in the far distance behind the trees in the centre of the photograph.

In this 1946 picture we are looking along Edinburgh Road from its junction with Stanhope Road on the right and the home of the *Portsmouth Evening News*.

In the centre of the road can be seen a redundant brick communal shelter, its days numbered. To the right of it can be seen the Portsmouth Coliseum of Varieties. This was demolished in the late 1950s and replaced by a Sainsbury's store. On the corner of Stanhope Road is Gale & Polden Ltd naval & military stationers & printers. In the 1960s the rooms above the shop were used as the naval recruiting office where your author was interviewed in December 1965, a fortnight after his fifteenth birthday, to join the Navy.

The large building opposite was at the time the Duchess of Albany Soldiers' & Sailors' Home. This building was later taken over by Aggie Weston's and became the Royal Sailors' Rest.

In the distance can be seen the gutted buildings of Commercial Road. Behind camera would be the railway gates protecting traffic from the dockyard branch railway line that crossed the road at this point.

There was also a Finlay & Co tobacconist and the silhouette shadow in the road was a sign above the kiosk stating 'Players Please'. This referred to Players cigarettes a popular brand of the time.

Looking along Edinburgh Road from its junction with Stanhope Road on the right circa 1946. The Portsmouth Coliseum is on the right middle distance.

The same vista today, little altered building wise, although the Coliseum has since been demolished.

Looking along Edinburgh Road today there is little change to the buildings although the Coliseum has long since been demolished. Sainsbury's built a supermarket on the site but it is now an Iceland frozen food centre. Gale & Polden also disappeared, the shop becoming a takeaway for some years. It was then a nail and beauty salon but is now a vacant shop and shuttered.

The naval recruiting office moved to new premises in Arundel Street but has since moved on from there. The Sailors' Rest also closed with the reduction in naval manning and became a homeless people's hostel with extra rooms built in the roof.

Here we see another view of the destroyed Bishop's House and the Roman Catholic Cathedral in Edinburgh Road after the rubble had been cleared and the road opened up once again. The hall has had its windows blown out and roof damaged. The white-painted trees bear witness to blackout regulations in force during the war years. I believe the brick building on the left could be a communal shelter but does not quite look high enough so I stand to be corrected. Out of camera on the left would be Victoria Park, the green lung of the city then as now.

The ruin's of the Bishop's House seen in the centre of the two buildings and shown earlier in the book on pages 78 and 79 from the opposite end of Edinburgh Road.

The Bishop's House has been rebuilt along with the hall. New trees complement the new buildings to make a fine screen, softening the harsh edges of the cathedral buildings. It is fanciful thinking but I wonder if one of the trees could be original?

The Bishop's House rebuilt along with the hall. New trees complement the new buildings and soften the sharp edges.

We are looking along Fountain Street off Edinburgh Road and opposite the Coliseum Theatre. The pub on the left was, at the time the photograph was taken, a beer house run by George Bowles. It later became the Shipwrights Arms and very popular. Alongside it to the left was the Trafalgar Services Club now a Wetherspoons Lloyds pub. Next along was the Park Hotel and then the extra popular Royal Standard. The landlady for many years was Ruby and any taxi driver worth his salt had better know where his fare was going when they asked 'Take me to Ruby's.'

Fountain Street off Edinburgh Road. Today's Balti House was once a pub called the Shipwrights' Arms.

Strange that when I took the modern photo workmen were repairing the old pub just as in the old photograph. The pub closed several years ago to become a takeaway. Wetherspoons who took over the Trafalgar Club still serves but is on the market at the time of writing. The Park Hotel now called the Park Tavern survives and Ruby's is just as popular. The building on the opposite corner of Fountain Street is now a betting shop more popularly called a 'bookies' by the locals.

Fountain Street today with the pub a long-gone memory and a betting shop on the opposite corner.

Taken from the steps of the gutted Portsmouth Guildhall behind camera, this is the view looking along Greetham Street to the left. It is amazing that after so much bombing, with the Guildhall left gutted after incendiaries fell onto the roof, that the buildings opposite remain almost untouched. The Sussex Hotel a once popular haunt of girls of the night remained in situ until the early seventies. Smarts was a furniture retailer with the slogan 'Easy to pay with the Smarts 4 years way'. Basically a hire purchase scheme.

This is a view across Guildhall Square from the steps of Portsmouth Guildhall.

Below is the vista one gets when standing on the Guildhall steps today. Every building seen in the previous photo was swept away in the early 1970s.

The tall building is the civic offices of the Portsmouth City Council. The modern pedestrianised square is popular for naval ceremonies.

You may not believe it but this is the same location today.

In this view taken from the same spot as the previous photograph, the cameraman has turned to his right and is looking south down Commercial Road.

The building to the right is the Portsmouth Gas Company offices. To the left are the Royal Insurance Building offices.

Further down Commercial Road can be seen the bomb site that was once the Hippodrome Theatre. Past that is Salem Street with the Primrose Milk Bar on the corner.

Opposite page: The same scene today with amazing changes. The former Portsmouth Gas Company has now become a branch of Wetherspoons pub chain. To the left,

the former insurance buildings have long gone and a library now occupies the site. The site of the former Hippodrome Theatre is now occupied by Hippodrome House, an office complex. The former theatre steps remained in situ until the rebuilding of the site in the 1980s. A long-lasting legacy from the war was discovered on 12 October, 1984. Workmen on the site uncovered a 500lb unexploded German bomb and the city centre had to be evacuated. The American comedian Bob Hope was due to appear at the Guildhall on the same evening and the show had to be cancelled. This part of the former Commercial Road is now called Guildhall Walk. The former milk bar on the corner of Salem Street, now out of view, is a pub which changes its name like the weather.

The cameraman has turned to his right and still looking from the Guildhall Steps we see Commercial Road.

The same vista today with trees in place of the lamp standard.

We are looking along Charlotte Street to its junction with Commercial Road. What was once a busy store is now all rubble protected by wooden boards.

Further up the street, the Monarch public house serves beer no more.

Charlotte Street looking towards the junction with Commercial Road. The public house at the end of the street is the Monarch.

The same scene today puts us at the junction of Eden Street which in turn leads on to Market Way. A discount store now owns the location of the former Monarch pub. The closed store on the corner of Eden Street tells its own tale of the fate of this once thriving street which was full of market traders from one end to the other. It is now but a ghost of what it was. What few barrow-boys there are these days do all their trade around the corner in Commercial Road.

Charlotte Street at the junction with Eden Street.

This is Raglan Street which used to run between Somers Road and Upper East Street where it became Greetham Street. In the distance is the brick wall dividing the roadway from the railway which lies at lower level in the former canal bed.

A wisp of steam can be seen escaping from a locomotive. To the right is the sign for the Raglan public house and the only pub in the street. It was located at number 31. In a later edition of Kelly's it tells us that in 1962, number 31 was the home of the Cleft Wing Youth Club and the Jehovah's Witnesses Kingdom Hall. To the left background can be seen houses in what I assume was Peckham Street with Omega Street Council School towering over them.

This is Raglan Street looking towards Greetham Street. On the right is the street's only pub, the Raglan.

The same scene today with my biggest problem on the right, large vehicles. I visited this location four times at different times of the day and there was always something parked in the same location. Behind the trees on the left can be just made out the former Omega Street School. It is now called the Omega Centre and deals with adult education.

A brighter picture with all the blitzed terraced house now gone and replaced by greenery.

If you could not see the clock tower of the Guildhall I don't suppose you would know where this photograph was taken. It is in fact at the top of Russell Street and going off to the left down to the White Swan public house in Commercial Road is Swan Street. The remains of the pub to the right of the man walking towards it was the Three Stags. There is not a lot more can be said about this photograph only that this all that remained of a once popular area of the city.

This is Russell Street from the corner of Upper Swan Street. The battered Guildhall clock tower overlooks the scene. In the left distance can be seen the White Swan public house with its mock-Tudor frontage.

Yes, the same scene today. The White Swan still survives in what is now Guildhall Walk. Another case of modern transport getting in the way, the white van man remained in situ for the whole hour I was on site. The Guildhall lost the top of the clock tower when it was rebuilt in the 1950s. The area is now a car park to the rear of the many pubs and clubs in what is now Guildhall Walk.

The same scene today. Unfortunately the delivery van remained parked in front of the White Swan for the whole hour I was on site.

The following two photographs are taken in the reverse location as to photographs on the previous pages. The photographer has walked along Russell Street and turned around to photograph the Three Stags from the opposite direction. To the right is Salem Street.

This would lead down to the rear entrance of the Hippodrome Theatre. The whole of this area is now a car park with Dorothy Diamond Street covering the Salem Street area.

This is a reverse of photographs on pages 102 and 103. To the right of the photo is Salem Street and we are looking at the Three Stags in Russell Street from the opposite direction.

The same scene today with Dorothy Diamond Street passing left to right in front of camera. It is a short cul-de-sac leading to the rear of Hippodrome House.

The mini with go-fast stripes on the left is at the same location as the picket fence in the older photograph. Swan Street passes along in front of the grey buildings.

The same view today and all change. The mini on the left is parked just about where the picket fence is in the older photograph.

Here we are looking west along New Road East at the junction with Northgate Avenue. The house on the corner has taken a direct hit. It was later demolished and a new property built on the site.

Notice the van turning into Percival Road on the right. Four cyclists can be seen in the road.

New Road East at the junction of Northgate Avenue. The enemy bombs struck far from any military location.

The same view today and all change, from the traffic point of view. Parked cars and vans are a curse to modern day street photographers.

It seems pointless waiting for some to move as they are replaced other vehicles immediately.

The site of the former bombed house is now a modern property set back somewhat from the pavement allowing the former General Stores bay windows to be seen.

New Road East today and the curse of the modern street photographer strikes in the form of so many cars parked in the street.

Ewart Road after the Luftwaffe had called again. The picture on the bedroom wall remains although the front of the room has been blasted out.

Just a single motor car is parked in the street. Two girls have a casual chat and a distant dog perhaps wonders where his next dinner is coming from?

Ewart Road, Copnor after the Luftwaffe had paid another visit. Notice the girl leaning against the lamp post talking to a friend and the dog in the distance.

Ewart Road today is all repaired. The only house looking different is the second one in from the left. Notice the woodwork under the eaves replaced as per the original.

The modern Portsmouth problem, cars, again defy the photographer to take a good picture.

Ewart Road today with repairs to the houses more or less exactly as they were before the bombing.

The once much-loved Palmerston Road which was an icon for the upper-crust of Southsea before the war now stands desolate.

In the distance can be seen the junction with Osborne Road. The photographer was standing in Grove Road South and to the immediate right is Kent Road.

What returning soldiers and sailors must have thought of this destruction after being away for several years can only be imagined.

Here we see a desolate Palmerston Road looking towards Osborne Road circa 1946. What was once a street of shops and fine houses now lies flat and protected by fencing

The same Palmerston Road in 2015 alive and full of shops of all kinds today.

It has since been pedestrianised with Grove Road South now making a sharp turn into Kent Road to pass the undamaged St Jude's church.

Palmerston Road reborn.

This is Alhambra Road, Southsea after a call from the Luftwaffe. One of the many fine town houses that used to stand along the road has been decimated.

Amazingly the Royal Beach Hotel on the seafront and which we can see the back of in the photo was untouched for the whole five years of the war.

Compared to today, the men removing the rubble have primitive working equipment, a crane with a bucket, a lorry that appears to take very little and men with ordinary clothes.

This is Alhambra Road, Southsea after a visit from the Luftwaffe. The large white building to the rear is the Royal Beach Hotel.

The same scene today and the fine house seen in the earlier photo has been demolished and an apartment block built in its place.

The Royal Beach Hotel, now called the Great Western Royal Beach Hotel, remains unscathed and one of the finest hotels in Southsea.

Front bedroom visitors have fine views across the Spithead and The Solent to the Isle of Wight.

Alhambra Road today.

King George VI and Queen Elizabeth during their many visits to the city during the war years.

King George VI, the Lady Mayoress and the Queen outside the Guildhall 6 February, 1941.

Here we see the Lord Mayor Denis Daly, the King and Queen, plus local dignitaries in Palmerston Road, Southsea, 6 February, 1941.

The Queen leads the King on an inspection of the Civil Defence at South Parade, Southsea 6 February, 1941.

The Rt Hon. Winston Churchill MP with the Lord Mayor of Portsmouth Denis Daly on a visit to the city 31 January, 1941.

*These final two photographs show the funeral cortege
and the graveside of some of the victims of the 10 January 1941 air raid.*

The funeral cortege trails along St Mary's Road before turning into Kingston Cemetery for the funeral of the victims of the air raid on the night of 10/11 January, 1941.

Ministers from all Faiths line the graveside of the communal burial of air raid victims from the 10/11 January blitz on the city.

Final Thoughts

The production of this book has been a labour of love on my part. Visiting parts of the city I rarely knew of and other areas that were key to my childhood it brought home to me what my parents and grandparents had to go through in those years of world war.

To all those who wondered why I was taking photographs of a blank scene, a car park, a memorial or of a street of no particular interest, within these pages lies your answer.

I must thank the editor Mark Waldron and the management of the *News* for allowing me to use the photographs from their publication *Smitten City*.

I must also thank Chief Reporter Chris Owen for assistance in obtaining information on several of the photographs by allowing me to place them in my Saturday column in the *News* more often than I am sure he would admit to liking. Thank you Chris.

I must also thank Anthony Triggs for the use of many of his photographs from his publication *Portsmouth – A Smitten City*.

Thank you Tony.

Many of the photographs in the book were so difficult to match after seventy years and with re-building on the locations it was a near impossible task at times.

Several of the photographs in the book I would have liked to have re-taken but unfortunately I was literally looking at a brick wall on many occasions!

I must thank the citizens of the city of who talked to me while I was on this project and who gave freely of their knowledge of certain locations.

Thank you one and all.

Robert W. Hind
November 2015